WORLD'S TALLEST DISASTER

Publication of this book was made possible by a generous grant
from the Greenwall Fund of The Academy of American Poets.

WORLD'S TALLEST
DISASTER

POEMS
Cate Marvin

WINNER OF THE 2000
KATHRYN A. MORTON PRIZE IN POETRY
SELECTED BY ROBERT PINSKY

Sarabande Books

LOUISVILLE, KENTUCKY

Copyright © 2001 by Cate Marvin

FIRST EDITION

Managing Editor
Sarabande Books, Inc.
2234 Dundee Road, Suite 200
Louisville, KY 40205

LIBRARY OF CONGRESS CATALOGING-IN-PUBLICATION DATA

Marvin, Cate, 1969–
    World's tallest disaster : poems / by Cate Marvin ; selected by Robert Pinsky.
        p.   cm.
    "Winner of the 2000 Kathryn A. Morton Prize in Poetry."
    ISBN 1-889330-60-4 (cloth : alk. paper) — ISBN 1-889330-61-2 (pbk. :
alk. paper)
    I. Pinsky, Robert. II. Title.

PS3563.A74294 W67 2001
811'.6—dc21   00-050478

This project was funded in part by a grant from the Kentucky Arts Council, a state agency of the Education, Arts, and Humanities Cabinet.

Cover painting: *World's Tallest Disaster* by Roger Brown. Provided courtesy of the Smithsonian American Art Museum.

Cover and text design by Charles Casey Martin

Manufactured in the United States of America
This book is printed on acid-free paper.

Sarabande Books is a nonprofit literary organization.

Special thanks are in order to Anonymous (2), The Murray and Grace Nissman Foundation, Anne Axton, Eleanor B. Miller, Jane Hamilton, Peter Saunders, and Jordan Miller.

*For Charles Burger Marvin
and Mary Jo VanKirk Marvin*

CONTENTS

Acknowledgments   ix
Foreword   xi

I

Reader, Please   3
The Anniversary   5
The Whistling Song from *Snow White*   8
Why Sleep   10
Me and Men   12
The Condition   13
House, Garden, Madness   15
Stopping for Gas near Cheat Lake   16
The Articulate   17
Mediterranean Blood Syndrome   19
Camp Rim Rock   21
Weather to Reel For   22
On Parting   24

II

Dear Petrarch   27
Mortal   28
Spell   30
Winter in Italy   32
The American   34
Alba: Aberdeen   36
The Tapestry   37
Dream on This   39
Pasture of My   41
Ekphrastic   42

Landscape Without You 44
Kansas 45
I Live Where the Leaves Are Pointed 47
Anathema 48

III

Please 53
Boiling Rocks 55
Discipline, Abandon 57
Ocean is a Word in This Poem 59
World's Tallest Disaster 60
Reading the New Sky 61
The Local Blind 62
The Negative Element 64
Breakfast in Bed 66
Spectacular 68
Cry Heard, Far Off 70
Cigarillo 71
The Readership 72

The Author 75

ACKNOWLEDGMENTS

Grateful acknowledgment is made to the editors of the following journals in which several poems in this collection have previously appeared:

The Antioch Review: "The Whistling Song from *Snow White*"; *Explosive Magazine*: "Breakfast in Bed"; *Gargoyle*: "The Local Blind"; *The Georgia Review*: "Please"; *Gulf Coast*: "Cry Heard, Far Off"; *New England Review*: "Cigarillo," "The Condition," "Weather to Reel For," "World's Tallest Disaster"; *The Paris Review*: "House, Garden, Madness," "Me and Men," "Mortal," "Reader, Please," "Stopping for Gas Near Cheat Lake"; *Ploughshares*: "I Live Where the Leaves Are Pointed"; *Post Road*: "Why Sleep," "Ocean is a Word in This Poem"; *Quarterly West*: "On Parting"; *Western Humanities Review*: "Alba: Aberdeen," "Anathema," "Dear Petrarch," "Kansas," "Spell"; *Witness*: "The Articulate," "Mediterranean Blood Syndrome"

The epigraph quotation by Ranier Maria Rilke is from "Antistrophes," in *The Selected Poetry of Ranier Maria Rilke*, Stephen Mitchell, trans., Vintage Books, 1989.

I am grateful for the guidance of Edward Hirsch, Richard Howard, Andrew Hudgins, and Adam Zagajewski. I am thankful for the friendship of Rick Barot, Andrew Brennan, Shannon Borg, Amber Dermont, Michael Dumanis, Kevin Honold, ZZ Packer, Jane Rosenzweig, Celeste Sheets, and Rebecca Wolff. I would also like to extend my heartfelt appreciation to Sarah Gorham, Jeffrey Skinner, and Robert Pinsky.

Violently passionate and firmly symmetrical, like tango or the
blues, these poems—at first—are about sexual passion. As in tango
or the blues, the geometry of form slices across the personal,
individual veins and muscles of Love itself, to reveal particular
truths. Cate Marvin's cunningly-measured, deceptively regular
stanzas partition the elegant dwelling where Eros like a wild ghost
bangs anyhow against walls or bursts across windowsill and
threshold. That dance or combat between form and passion makes
an immediate impact in the characteristic poems of *World's Tallest
Disaster*. Even the title, with its cool, comic invocation of a shock-
TV copywriter's idiom, turns that hackneyed form around by
alluding—in all three words—to extremes: the global and
superlative extravagances of burning love.

But in the great tradition of love poetry, these poems don't
stop with love. They move from Eros to imagination. Or they
thrash between the two, in a progress that takes them up above
through torch song, through sonneteer's hyperboles of
complaint, toward the mysteries of the self's need to imagine an
other.

I mean, for example, the way the sentences rave across the
quatrains of "The Articulate," the breaking down into body parts
not so much analytical as explosive:

> Mean-fisted, sterilized with alcohol,
> gray in its cage of ribs, my heart
> speaks to my stomach. *How do you find
> yourself now, with the constant stinging*
>
> *of whiskey and no food, how is it to close
> on such sharpness and emptiness?*
> Stomach groans, tired of patience.
> Whole gut recalls the cleanliness

of youth, when it eavesdropped on Feet
complaining, while Brain maintained
a certain courtesy in argument. Even
then, the Heart was not nice.

This game is so boldly played that it recalls the free-swinging
metaphors of George Herbert or Philip Sidney, that nerviness of
poetry in English when it was new. Perhaps many young poets
might take up an idea like this, but nearly all would leave it cute or
preening, or wrap it up too easily. Cate Marvin sustains it, folds it
and extends it. Here are some lines from a bit later on in the poem:

Even now, the innards talk. And the Heart
has often been caught in lies. None
of the body likes him. If he were not tucked

safe in a cavity, if he were not so embedded,
they would reject him. Even Eyes wish
they did not have to feed him vision.

And the poem ends with a kind of surprise return of the first
person, and with a sense of revelation right through the final
three words:

Like Eyes,
I have a part in it, but I do not recommend
flesh as a means of transport to anyone.

Even the novel sensation of Hands
on the skin is not worth it. Alarmed at touch,
the muscle clutches blood, refusing delirium.
And to kiss or question, Mouth is mute.

The concluding assertion of muteness, paradoxical after such
rhetorical acrobatics, caps the movement from the mere pathos of
one lovestruck to the active, pained engagement of imagination.
From self-pity, to self-display, to a transcendent alertness: that is
the course of love poetry reaching beyond its banalities, and
Marvin follows that course with her own, idiosyncratic zest.

This is an encouraging book in the context of American poetry's fashions or factions, because it evades categories. More inventive than ploddingly narrative, more passionate than merely self-reflexive, these poems don't feel like they spring from any literal or figurative school, but from the kinds of knowledge and self-knowledge, evasion and rage, invoked by the volume's epigraph from Rilke. In these live and engaging poems, Cate Marvin has earned the meaning of the epigraph and the privilege of citing Rilke—and of entitling a poem "Dear Petrarch." That poem begins with the Italian poet's line *"The sweet singing of virtuous and beautiful ladies"* and ends: "Lots of ladies sing along to the radio / now. But the hole of our mouths holds a howl." The line with its figures of sound both parodies and acknowledges the way poetry can thrive on anger, pleasure, and need. This is an urgent as well as an artful voice.

—*Robert Pinsky*
July, 2000

Wir, von uns selber gekränkt,
Kränkende gern und gern
Wiedergekankte aus Not.
Wir, wie Waffen, dem Zorn
neben den Schlaf gelegt.

We, afflicted by ourselves,
gladly afflicting, gladly
needing to be afflicted.
We, who sleep with our anger
laid beside us like a knife.
—Rainer Maria Rilke

I

READER, PLEASE

You didn't light my cigarette.
Offered your lighter so I could light it myself.
Recall the white room I took you to
when you could not breathe?
Reader, please, it's called chivalry.

Five years you've lived since that night
and you won't offer a flame?
You lay purple in the emergency
room, stuttering on the syllable of your name.
To think I actually prayed.

When the blood drained from your face,
you rose new and strange, a white flower.
Your leaving felt like atrocity.
I should not have said it.
Yes, you, as one loves a saint.

Let us speak of that other night,
how the moon struck the sky with its sickle
and we lay as two halves in a decrepit
hotel room in New France,
let us order more whiskey.

Reader, it was the funniest thing—
after you left I stood in the parking lot,
leaned back against a parked car, smoking.
Reader, they called security.
A uniformed man appeared in the doorway.

The light from his flashlight traveled
over me—exposed, derelict.
He approached me cautiously,

Ma'am, are you a guest here?
I nodded soberly, though the whole night

shook me till I was so dizzy
I laughed. Your eyes are like hands
dipped in blue paint, they grab and grab.
Sometimes, reader, I wish they'd taken
me away, right there and then.

THE ANNIVERSARY

I.

Disappointment with the lack of stars.
Where's the moon when I call it?
Perhaps it's not up to being the color
I want tonight: bloody orange, peeling light.

Five sick summers that I've slept
with a dream for lover: Hands raw,
knuckles white on the wheel's ring,
he winds blindly South, eyes licked

by sunset, their blue lapped. The moon
crawls like a snail up the sky's wall.
Waking, I find its trail faint as the trace
of chalk erased from a blackboard.

But tonight I call myself Destination.
As he sinks into bed, pillow exhaling
the weight of his head, I circle the edge
of his dream, clutching my invitation.

Department of stars, I address whoever's
in charge: Why haven't you responded
to my queries on brightness? I only ask
that you appear sharply for this occasion.

II.

Limbs entirely too still, branches retracted.
Docile as indoor cats, they startle nothing.
Are the trees afraid to enact the scene
I desire? His breath's intake, sudden gash.

One thousand eight hundred twenty five
nights that I've crouched in this dream's
hedge, stalking his attention. Face pressed
at a window so dark I've learned nothing.

Once I crept through a graveyard, dug
his mother up to ask her where he went.
She said he'd gone to the movies. Another
drama, not good enough, my drama—

If I wasn't always dreaming his cast-call,
could I forget our anniversary? I audition
dutifully. Though years have smeared
my mouth red, its bloody seam still sings!

Officer of trees, when will our meeting
convene? Will your limbs shake as agreed,
or do you need a more detailed explanation?
I only ask that you tap his window lightly.

III.

One night before the moon ate all of me
I woke and went outside. Above the fogged
definition of skyline, I saw a bit of myself,
slivered. For hours I tried to take it back.

My love, wherever he was, slept. Tonight
that won't suffice. No, it won't do to have
him or the moon absent on this occasion.
Not when I've chosen the sky we'll meet

under this last time. I draped this cloud's
amorous gauze, and combed the soft grass
where we'll lie. I wear his eyes like rings
on my hands. I sew the years into a dress.

We'll drive back to the motel that shone
its lights to us the rainy night, the last
night I slept where he slept. The quiet room
where my eye last closed on his cloudy eye.

Moon, don't forget your allegiance. Gold
as a trumpet's mouth, or strange as a siren—
wear whatever light you like. I don't care,
just hang yourself loud enough to wake him.

THE WHISTLING SONG FROM
SNOW WHITE

When I was little in a large room,
a large blue room, I listened over and over
to that record—-the whistling song
my favorite tune. Little and listening

to that whistling tune over and over,
I danced around a huge sombrero,
thinking about how one boy said
he would marry me. They said

I could be a fireman or President,
if I wanted. In this country. Funny,
now I've got my own country.
A small land of paper piling.

Here, the mountains are like breasts,
but I discourage building, I forbid zoning.
I say, Wear that tight red dress.
I say, Wear that short slip.

I command, Make yourself look
like you want to get fucked.
Because in my land, no one gets
fucked over. It's not like a nudist

colony, where flesh rolls as arms reach
for glasses by the swimming pool.
Jaws open, vulvas fly like birds.
No one ever says, Why'd you wear

a dress like that, cut so low to show
off your breasts? There are no breasts here.

8

There are mountains and there are groves,
exotic plants you could liken to cunts.

But I won't allow that context.
If you're my subject you walk a while,
you like scenery. You are not a man
or a woman. Your mind feels, your body

thinks—mine thinks back now to the blue
room, the beaten brim of that sombrero;
my feet bare and the whistle of that tune
dragging its needle along my ear's tunnel.

WHY SLEEP

I might miss something. The man who paces
his dog as my eyes walk with him between the slats
of blinds. The neighbor girl who always wakes
me anyhow with her cry, *You're such an asshole!*

And I've been inclined to agree since I heard
him tell her one four a.m. he hoped she'd die.
I might miss the nice blue and red flashing the cop's
car makes on the blind, as it hums outside—

as I strain to make out this low murmur, *But she locked
me out, Sir.* And I would not get to see the lovely
orange that will take this place down—and it will,
eventually, with all the gas pouring from my stove's

unlit pilot—Lovely, lovely flames! I want to watch
them consume us—and then I'd still be awake, standing
out on the chilly street, having saved myself, and having
saved myself I'd have to watch everything but me

go down. And don't I care for the neighbor girl?
Maybe I'd save her. I thought of taking a cake,
or some tea, down there tonight. But I was too afraid
she'd come to her door with an array of bruises

I'd have to address. Sleep? Those bruises are hers,
not mine. I lie, I lie. Here, inside the beat, deaf even
to the beat, only able to be the beat: muscle, muscle,
heart, thighs. When the cop car goes away, he stays.

And then there's another sort of cry. In the morning,
I rise ringy eyed—and I suppose I rummage
through nights like a raccoon, too, having to sort
out the rotten from the rotten. This night's food satisfies;

day's a porridge that will suffice. And what's there
to say in that plain light, when I see him out walking
the dog? Hello, hello—sorry about the disturbance
last night. *I must have slept through it,* I lie.

ME AND MEN

The soiled fists of socks shucked before
   they fell lumbersome to bed, the dirty pans,
      the glasses their lips kissed fisted soapy
in my sink-worn hands. The flea-seeded sink,
   basin of stubble shorn, their low snores
      rumbling nights long as freight trains.

True, some nights their eyes pooled with light,
   cleared to brown, unmuddied their river bottoms.
      But more often, I liked best not being with them,
   driving alone and thinking only of the fact of them.
      Their flat bodies I held with grave disrespect;
         perhaps this is why I sought them.

There were shadows beneath their eyes, and sweet
   and slow moments unzipping their flies. I may
      have gasped from time to time. But it is unfortunate,
for my men, that they knew me, and I knew them
   as men. My blankness should have never
      had anything to do with them. I tried

to forgive them for dropping their dirty clothes
   by the bed, for playing deaf to my questions,
      for ashing on my favorite rug, for slamming doors
on my hands, for being them. I can't blame them
   for owning what I wanted, back when
      what I wanted was had only by men.

If I can't wish a scar away, how can I wish them
   obliviated from my touching? The fact is,
      I am unable to remember their faces, any
of them, the smell of their collars, the fury I felt,
      why I broke and broke things. It all seems quite bland,
         and I would rather think of animals I have had.

THE CONDITION

for Rebecca

What we share most is boredom, friend,
        as we walk depraved the graveyards
of supermarket aisles, noting the dearth
        of interesting men. In the bright light,

the dead bright light, our eyes fasten
        on the new produce boy. When we hold
out a bulb of Spanish garlic to ask him,
        Why purple? he does not understand

what we find exotic and answers dumbly,
        It tastes the same as the plain variety.
And so he escapes becoming a topic
        for our perverse conversation. And what

do we want, that we must discuss men
        with such fervor? *I like younger ones,*
I like the blond one, I like him, no, him.
        Our conversation seamless, not stitched

with awkward silence, we simply like
        the act of eying. Did you note his thighs,
his quartzlike eyes, or were you looking
        at another guy? Then the talk defaults

to our other favored topic: death. Not dying
        in a metaphorical sense. We lay our words
like tenuous plats, build a bridge over its
        unthinkable depth: Not a sea of longing,

but the brack of wanting what's physical
        to help us forget we are physical. We walk

in pants, but live in bodies termed feminine,
    stalking bright aisles in search of distraction.

HOUSE, GARDEN, MADNESS

Meeting his mouth made it so I had house again.
I called him garden and drew him so, grew
his long lashes like grasses so I could comb
them with my stare. Some evenings a low cloud
would arrive, hang its anxiety over the yard.

Having his mouth at mine again gave me back
home. The walls painted themselves blue,
flowers grew larger than my head, stared
at me with wide eyes through the windows.
I was surrounded. A cloud stretched gray arms.

His mouth and mine again built something back
up with heat. The house was home again, wherever
I lived. The flowers grew fat, fed on weeds
around them. Ladybugs tucked their red luck
beneath petals' chins. The cloud came home again.

His eyes were closed but mine kept swinging open.
I saw him in the garden, surrounded by its light.
The flowers cut their own stalks, handed themselves
over to him in bunches. He kissed their bouquets,
and petals raptured. A cloud lowered, dark with fury.

I pressed my mouth to palm, closed my eyes
to find the garden, then saw: windows shut in fright,
roots drowned, flower stalks broken, their heads dead
in puddles. Startled, I looked around. The cloud
descended, prepared to hemorrhage in my arms.

STOPPING FOR GAS NEAR CHEAT LAKE

Trees bent unnatural by wind,
then frozen, looking delicate as jewelry, but unwearable.
Miles of white, palest skin,
and the slash of the road through it. Who named this lake,

who lost? How clear is its water
when not frozen? Do the townspeople refuse to swim in it,
or is it a site for seasonal pleasures?
At the self-serve station, the man insists on filling my tank.

Has everybody in town lost
their money, what can I buy to save them? A cigarette lighter,
a hunter's cap, windshield fluid...
some of my blood's origin is here—a family with white gums

and skin blue as this dusk.
Something not right about it—one year they tested vials
over and over. The doctors:
You'll need to come in again; your blood is strangely thin.

What do you know of your heritage?
The houses are red on Fairchance Lane, their windows look
away from the banks of the lake,
tree-shaded places where lovers embraced. I could stop

the car, stand in those shadows,
and try to find my face on the surface of Cheat Lake.
Or I could walk into town, find
my reflection in the eyes of a distant cousin, lead him

to the water's edge, my white face
haunting him. For those who drowned, for those who escaped,
I demand an answer. Tell me,
tell me where I can find the bastard who named this lake.

THE ARTICULATE

Mean-fisted, sterilized with alcohol,
gray in its cage of ribs, my heart
speaks to my stomach. *How do you find*
yourself now, with the constant stinging

of whiskey and no food, how is it to close
on such sharpness and emptiness?
Stomach groans, tired of patience.
Whole gut recalls the cleanliness

of youth, when it eavesdropped on Feet
complaining, while Brain maintained
a certain courtesy in argument. Even
then, the Heart was not nice. Encumbered

with ache and claustrophobia, his speeches
grew especially loud when the night woke
and wolf-curtains drew shut. We lay
very small in that room, certain the curtain's

pattern grew into a jungle of red eyes
glaring out from darkness. Heart resented
cramped quarters; Brain attempted
to maintain an even discourse. Parts

of my body had parts, played out a sort of play.
Even now, the innards talk. And the Heart
has often been caught in lies. None
of the body likes him. If he were not tucked

safe in a cavity, if he were not so embedded,
they would reject him. Even Eyes wish
they did not have to feed him vision.
They would have closed on the drunk

so sallow on a corner if they did not
have to look at the road to drive. Like Eyes,
I have a part in it, but I do not recommend
flesh as a means of transport to anyone.

Even the novel sensation of Hands
on the skin is not worth it. Alarmed at touch,
the muscle clutches blood, refusing delirium.
And to kiss or question, Mouth is mute.

MEDITERRANEAN BLOOD SYNDROME

Vials of my weakness. Five fingers, black-red.
    Tubes of my dizziness. *Look, your face,*
your hands, their paleness. Have I or any of my
    blood relatives ever had *shortness of breath?*

While climbing stairs? Tightness in your chest?
    Which awakens you at night? When walking
against a wind? What is your heritage?
    I ought to watch my blood if I marry

Mediterranean. *The trait's often carried by*
    those of that descent. Marriage of disaster,
blood's weakness. They say if I have you, child,
    they'll have to shine lights on your skin

day and night to keep it from yellowing.
    But I always knew my family white
as the sun looked head on: Scots-Dutch, blue
    gums, lungs black as coal mines,

pale faces shining out from Pennsylvanian
    pitch—those mountains sawed in half
to make roads, and grandmother's mad eyes
    on her deathbed, marble clear and awfully

blue until her end. I haven't met your father yet,
    but doctors demand we never put our cells
together—if we do, we'll make you. I know
    I should not have you, but knowing

you would die if I did makes me want you
    to live. *It would be an unpleasant life,*
the doctor said, despite medical advancements.
    Needled flesh, hourly transfusions . . .

I never thought myself mother, but now you're
          leaving me all the time, you leave me again,
yellow child with the tired grin. Not able to be
          your mother, I dream for us a bloodless heaven.

CAMP RIM ROCK

To furnish the memory's wood with trees:
thick and huddled about Danielle crouched
close to the gleam of her new pocketknife,
her hands raw from their lack of dexterity.
              What shape did she hope to make?
      Whittled unneatly, sawed with frustration,

the stick lay quietly in her skinned hands.
She folded the knife, wiped a rusty smear
across her brow absently. Danielle's mustard
colored hair, her predatory stare, finding
              myself caught in its cross-hairs.
      She dragged me off to help

her trap frogs, their embodied dissection
following. Those thick days I hid from her
in the archery shack, mealtimes I crept through
the line with my tray. Danielle's hair yellow
              as the sand dumped by the river's
      edge to make pretend it was a beach.

Shrouded in thick trees, she lurked dangerously.
Communal showers, outhouse stink, whir
of heavy insects, Danielle's face appearing
in the tiny window of the archery shack.
              Arrows were hung on a hanging rack.
      I slept those nights afraid of children,

among bunks of sleeping children. For all
the trees thick on that mountain, there was no
place to hide. All the eyes following me inside
the archery shack. The cabin filled with the breath
              of scheming children. The night still
      terrifies, the night and her many children.

WEATHER TO REEL FOR

I.

You could have wasted someone
else's time, but you chose mine, darling,
and I'll never regret those nights lying
like an organ separate and packed in ice, on a flight
     to the failing patient who needed me most.

     Forest of feeling, bell within my body
reeling, a memory prized as a prized
horse, it kept me going, dragged me up
to call the sky, roil it into my weather, nearly
     always tornado. Five years near and dear

     as the day you nearly died. Used to be
your mention, a forehead creased as yours,
could pivot the heart. The flamed tissue
of an orange begonia budding within the screened
     porch—its fierceness of color I admired.

     I remember that afternoon as well
as I remember five years, orange flowers aglow,
the only alive as I sat smoking. And with what
chilly pleasure I knew my being without
     desire to lift your name, caw it to fame—

     was grateful as a victim of natural disaster,
glad the tornado had stopped scouring.
Though cows are still sick with fear, will not
stop lowing, though the house still lies in shards
across pastures, some fifty miles away.

II.

The sky righted itself, struck the town
down with dawn. Houses smashed
flat, I walked streets fuming.
                                    Streets
eased beneath my feet, slid greased
paths beneath me. Houses looked sad
on their sides, flat and fuming.
With the stench of squashed inhabitants,
                                    I walked towns
fuming, posed flame bright by a bridge
I'd have crossed if I hadn't thrown
it to a river—
                        whose silver silence always moved away
anyway. I didn't especially care
about all I'd lost, wanting
but not knowing what,
                                    the streets cluttered
with dead houses. Too bright, that morning—
then the thing (we call it *sky*) lowered,
drawing its orange arm across the land
and smearing us off the plains—O, drama.
                        Your red sun which never
                        sets but has kept
                        my hide burnt with wakefulness.
                                    I will flee
to a store to buy more cigarettes—
and you and I and you and I again,
                        blooming up
into the sky's eye again. Orange sucking flower,
pulling my day into its fire, I will stand alone,
smeared with the pollen of your
                        day's new heat.
        Like a dog longing
to please its master, I lick your sweet damage.

ON PARTING

Before I go let me thank the man who mugs you,
taking your last paycheck, thank the boss who steals
your tips, thank the women who may break you.

I thank the pens that run out on you midsentence,
the flame that singes your hair, the ticket you can't
use because it's torn. Let me thank the stars

that remind you the eyes that were stars are now
holes. Let me thank the lake that drowns you, the sun
that makes your face old. And thank the street your car

dies in. And thank the brother you find unconscious
with bloody arms, thank the needle that assists in
doing him in—so much a part of you. No thanks

to the skin forgetting the hands it welcomed, your
hands refusing to recall what they happened upon.
How blessed is the body you move in—how gone.

II

DEAR PETRARCH

The sweet singing of virtuous and beautiful ladies...
More like dogs barking, more like a warning now.
When our mouths open the hole looks black,
and the hole of it holds a shadow. Some keep

saying there's nothing left to tell, nothing to tell.
If that's the truth I'll open my door to any
stranger who rattles the lock. When my mouth
opens it will scream, simply because the hole

of it holds that sound. As for your great ideas,
literature, and the smell of old books cracked—
the stacks are a dark area, and anyone could find
herself trapped, legs forced, spine cracked.

It's a fact. Everyone knows it. If I lived in your
time, the scrolls of my gown would have curled
into knots. It's about being dragged by the hair—
the saint, the harlot both have bald patches. Girls

today walking down the street may look sweet,
chewing wads of pink gum. And the woman at the bar
may never read. Lots of ladies sing along to the radio
now. But the hole of our mouths holds a howl.

MORTAL

How do you find yourself in literature?
All blue eyed, drinking from green bottles.

Do you think I've done the sky right?
Or was it cloudier than blue? The canoe

is as thin as I can make it: a dry
stick hollowed to make a flute. Could you

think of something more appropriate?
Here, you make some noise with it.

Oh, famous. A tall building swept into
the Mississippi that month of flooding,

roofs like hats floating. Your flat world
then, so green and swaying, wet with muck,

fish too caught in current to be spawning.
Should I have something about dresses

in the wind, their white skirts waving?
Once you're dry in Kansas, don't think

of thanking me. Don't come to the bar
to find me years later, when I'm bound

to drink's dark spiral, strapped in the same
way to that boat as the still Lady was

when she floated down the river's dim
expanse. Gather, instead, with the rest

of the town at the edge of the harbor.
Or find out about it later in the paper, along

with other reports of death and torture.
This won't be the last the world reads of you.

SPELL

There is a couch, a chair, a table.
A glass of wine on the table.

Tonight I'm tall and white
with a mouth red from wine.
You've seen me walk
through rooms like this:

by a couch, a chair, to a table
to reach for a glass of wine.

In that town a small room,
old with the smell of wood,
had fires inside and snow thick
on cars below the window.

Here, nights thrum with insects,
pebbled stairs crawl with ants.

My stare's the same in any weather.
Let's choke back another
glass, let's not gasp
when you enter the room.

You, thick on drink, stand inches away.
In the light of this kitchen, we cook.

The wine stains your mouth purple,
like mine. In our old time, the spirits
were pure. Whiskey straight
from the bottle—

Let us sit down to the table:
thick on drink, common in hunger.

I won't stroke your hair,
touch your breath with my tongue.
Your clothes come undone.
We are the friends we always

had been. The droplets
on your mouth.

WINTER IN ITALY

You are dogs with rhinestone collars,
        you are pelts adorning women,
you have violent means of making
        me see myself. You are this white
sheet, are the father of my children,
        you call my blood back, say
it's no good. *This is how you will
        have it?* I'll send myself back
in a letter. Our picture together.
        By now you are summer in Africa.

When you are summer in Africa
strange animals ask that you forget us:
        those confused streets, sewage
swollen canals, baroque expressions
        dismal with history. Our murky
city, stupor of cloud, the unintelligible
        currency, words I tripped over,
how you found me unnavigated, why
        we fought over the map, when
we stood alone and bereft by fountains.

Someone who knew a lover in Italy
        also called it a cloak, the sky—said
it was azure, unrolling, roiling,
        predictably glorious, the sky. Sad,
you would have me call it circus,
        the sky's grotesquerie of cloud,
rain's pelt and always your sore
        foot, us locked in a room where
we lay all afternoon on the bed
        staring up at the ceiling's lid. I do

not think I betrayed you intentionally.
It was not my thinking of other eyes—
    but did I tell you? Someone who also
knew a lover in Italy called it azure,
    that blue heat, that widening of sky,
the tiny struggles of happiness beneath.
    May I call you Winter in Italy? I saw
a moon there catch fish with its glowing,
    snapping jaws. And there are many
books to write beneath calmer lights.

THE AMERICAN

I didn't cross the ocean to read *Anna Karenina*
on your green couch too fat with cushions.
You're out back hanging laundry. Most
of the time, you're out back hanging laundry.

You'd take me to see sites, but I'm sick
of Roman ruins and castles bore me now.
The fish store across the street stinks—
come to think, the whole town stinks.

You live so close to the oil-clogged sea,
I've been looking around for a gangplank.
I mention liking dogs so you will take me
to the country where your sister has three,

where she and your parents live meagerly,
operating a tea shop somewhere in the hills
where no one ever comes to eat. Your mother
offers a baked potato, a filled roll—the unvaried

menu of your country. Your father talks politics.
I wonder if you're sick of me? Your sister's
glasses are so fogged and scratched it's a wonder
she can see as she yells at one of her dogs,

Laddie, stop chasing the sheep! I came here
with my brief sense of history. I dislike how you
eat what's on your plate. Those powdered eggs,
the stiff fluff of old rolls you tear open to butter.

The murk of your city. Don't you wonder why
I nap so much in the day? The hills are simmering
and the dogs have run off. I'm beginning to think
I'll never get away. The moment you put your head

to the pillow, I'm up with a drink to cure my headache.
The husband you don't touch glances at me.
What, I wonder, do you dream as we walk off
to kiss and loll by edge of the reeking sea?

ALBA: ABERDEEN

A sky that blue is not a sad thing.
Some nights are not worth sleeping. And knowing
we'll never see a blue like that

ever again is fine. There are
nights not worthy of sleep. When the blue brims
like that and swallows the town

in its huge tear, the little
bridges we walk back over leave us. We're almost
back at your house, so we sit

in the alley and wait a while
for the sky to become normal. Our mouths marry
in smoke and the aftertaste

of Scotch. A man walks by
with his dog. Gulls shriek and dive; their noises
are terrible; the town wakes.

We pace some more before
returning each other's hands, then decide to sleep
the day. Your wife is waking

for work. We are almost
asleep, in our separate rooms. Our lungs are blue
from breathing that color.

Our faces wear the same
expression. The sky is incapable of anything bluer.
Our hearts cannot be redder.

THE TAPESTRY

completed, knotted at the ends. No unraveling there,
not even teeth could tear those fine, firm stitches.
Its story now hangs in the world as a bird's call
seems to hang in a valley forever. The grass looks soft
as hair, the river bends like a limb through the field,
meets a lake that threatens to drown you with its stare.

No one must know.

Having been there before and written home about it,
having bound the account even, and sold it to friends
and passers-by, what point was there in my returning?
No use in returning after turning it into an account.
One hoped every event had found its place; one led
each event to its place card in the vast room of story.

No one must know you've made this.

A mystery solidly unsolved as those ships sunk
to unbreathable depths. There was no leniency for
mutability there. Even its air was rock solid, pretty
and hazed as a crystal. Sometimes you could see a bit
of your hand, the pink of a finger, through it. Now,
one discerns a beat, senses heat, a live thing waiting.

Except for him.

What has it done to change my city? Inchoate, I stare
at the shimmering: towers turned night objects, human
landscape, immovable and beautiful. In the mailbox,
a scrawl I know. That country's postmark. Some

deep-set, rusted thing breaks open, releasing an ocean of revisable truth. Now where will the story go?

Except, perhaps, for him.

DREAM ON THIS

*Researchers in Scotland have developed a
technique for cloning unlimited numbers of
genetically indistinguishable sheep.*
—Houston Chronicle, 1996

Near the city of granite buildings, the block of houses he grew
in, the house his parents still live in, the rooms he shares
with her body, the rooms she painted green as a clean sea,

where she stands wiping the kitchen counter down as the small
washing machine turns his worn clothes over and over, the lines
strung out back where his pants dry, stiff with detergent, hanging

next to a sheet he will sleep on, next to her body, somewhere near
his radium city, cells divide repeatedly in culture dishes.
They start with the embryo and watch its red unfold until—

here's a picture of their identical heads; rough hands grasp
    their necks,
hold their bodies so the noses touch for the camera. Twin
    eyes side
by side, each curved at the edge like a smile. As his life occurs

next to hers, I am unfolding the paper, taking a crushed cigarette
from its pack. I light it and turn the pages on the world, smoking.
The caption below the heads says, *The endless stream of identical*

sheep insomniacs envisioned has become a reality. At a cafe
in his city I once sat, listened across a table as he lamented the loss
of individuality. *Only five identical lambs have been created so far;*

three died in the first days of life. Am I too weak to produce
an analogy? Such a minor success—*The Scottish are so miserable,
always complaining,* he was saying. When I was his America,

a loving destiny, what was I thinking as I lay in that city, gulls
swooping near the window at dawn, their noise hating sleep,
and that sea-green room swallowed me? That near the store

where he stocked shelves all night when he was broke and fifteen,
near the bridge he hid us beneath to quiet our speech,
    somewhere not far
from where her body lay asleep, cells divided. As her head fell

to the pillow, he and I stood by the shadowed water, our hands
fastening on the word *Always*. The cells are growing, in
    that room
he is moving, hands twisting in her hair as if caught in flame.

Before a drop of water sweating from my drink smears the
    paper's ink,
before I rise and walk away from the cigarette's smoky wreath,
I read that *mated cells are zapped with an electric current.*

Their bodies team in my dreams, join, leap fences.

PASTURE OF MY

Ire field, long running with flame grass:
what can I untell you? Even the weeds have
eavesdropped. And you, incapable of misstep,
make fronds cringe with your scrutiny. Sorry,
my field says, that you have passed through
us at wrong hours, sorry that when sun lights
upon us we grow tawdry with flame. Why

is it always my field, my grass, my thin
creek running blue wire through my being?
Only my and mine, my and my own, always
the swerving grain I've known. Still, would
you exist if not for patience, if not for waiting—
and cycles long we have waited for your
singular tread. Still, we worry you'll find

our green not stunning enough, find us in
our wanting, wanting. Perhaps you'll lean
to twist a flower from its stem, then find your
hand touches nothing, perhaps you won't,
perhaps we do not exist. Still, it makes us be,
your walking through us—and all the years
we lay beneath weather passively, we forget.

EKPHRASTIC

I hung the painting of the scary forest
        so I could always be running through it.
Though no one told me how at first,
        by now I know the way out: I learned it.
The stalks of trees he swept on a page
        with clean strokes of ink were first neat—
but then he made leaves, underbrush
        with his quill's sharp tip. He scribbled
brambles, smeared dark holes, patches
        with the blunt tip of his index finger.
A skillful painter with a rage colorful
        as his palette, he employed inks and oils
with equal talent, but chose just black
        for this forest. In the same room bright
with windows, in which he conceived
        this landscape, he once took my head,
shook it like a rattle. On the white wall,
        my skull dented letters he'd read later.
His brush was deft, his intent a mallet.
        I am escaping again, breathless—his stare
scares the tongue right out my mouth,
        shells my face so its teeth fall like pearls.
Only I can see the red in this picture.
        (His mouth's bow tied in a smile, butterfly
kisses under a tree he painted to hide
        us beneath so my mother wouldn't find out.)
He's trapped me again with the wet muck
        of his brush, stabs my foot with his quill.
I pick my body up and jump a familiar
        hurdle—the thick log fallen in the foreground.
Though I drop to the other side, I am
        not safe—his stained hand catches my ankle.
I swipe at it, bash his tender nails with
        my closed fist. Smearing the frame as I grasp

its edge, I haul myself over, fall back
            to my room's bare walls. Shaking, I draw
my arm across my mouth, then stare
            at the bloody seam my lip's left. The sea sighs,
a branch cracks as if thrown by waves
            against land's barrier. Across an ocean, he
drops his palette, shakes off scales of skin
            and charred letters. He has just managed
to find his way out of this poem again.

LANDSCAPE WITHOUT YOU

Roofers scrape the scaly lid
of an auto shop beside the house
where I live. Where I live
shirtless men tear at the black

scabs of a roof's old flesh, toss
scraps into the back of a truck
parked in the lot next to a house
where I live. Where I live

a tarp rattles at night, plastic
rustles, and trash is kicked along
pavement by wind. Roofers
curse and shell the tire shop's

peeling lid beside the house
where I live. Where I live
a tarp shakes all night; cans
land on pavement, tossed from

windows of cars that blur by
where I live. Where I live
windows are ladled red with
light your sun leaves me with.

Repairs are made to roofs which
will never cover me. As I read
the road between us, tire tracks
unscroll their tawdry calligraphy.

Any day now you shall arrive, roar
into my eye with your mountainside.
Where I live when I live where
landscape cannot survive you.

KANSAS

A hair in the throat.
A lash in the eye.
What a washing down,
what a washing out.

The tree sticks in my throat
like a bone, the building sticks
to my eye like an icicle to tongue.
Your gate, iron-wrought.
The walk drags my feet along it.

Stairs trip me up them. Red brick
bleeds on my hands, prints its touch
with rust. The knob bends my fingers
back. The door slams me in.
To return to, to return to—

an air tinged with blizzard. A still
leaky tap clinking at a stack
of dirty dishes. The red rug laps me
at you, lolls me up your corridor.
My hands are raw from wind.

Your rings have sawed my fingers.
Strange, I always thought if we
were to again meet, it would be
in Paradise: shorn of skin, deboned,
rinsed from our bodies.

Our winter is done, the heart
gnawed to none, yet it seems I must
still watch you pick your teeth
with its bone. You might
have known I'd come home.

My throat full of burrs.
My eyes stuck with dust.
All the washing down.
All the washing out.

I LIVE WHERE THE LEAVES ARE POINTED

at my head and my heart, knife-tips green
in a gasoline-doused garden. From the tire
store behind the house, leering mechanics
glaze my window with saliva. I sit at the end
of the couch and point my finger angrily,
wag it in the face of forever. I sit back on
my haunches and sniff the air. Please note:
the earth is no less sulfur than usual. It's not
nothing I'm waiting for, not as if there's no
reason I've done my hair at last. If I weren't
waiting, why would I be so impatient?
I don't drink whiskey to relax.
And there is someone I wouldn't mind seeing
dead. But when I comb my hair and stay
up all night, it's not as if I'm trying to meet
someone. The days can travel without me.
The landlord can mow the lawn in shifts,
his pink face an obscene balloon caught
by the noose of his collar—I'll sleep through
the motor. And you can bet my dreams bloom
stranger than hallucination. I take my life
like this. Poems grow from my skull while
vines creep the tire store wall: slowly, certainly.
When they made soap, they had me in mind.

ANATHEMA

I never recline in splendor,
I never take repose. The eyes
of an old woman are blue
and stick to me like insects to
a screen. She is not hating me,
though there are those who hate me,
so I never lie in repose for fear
that if I agree with the vulnerability
of sleep, I'll make my own murder.

I don't embrace the unconscious
or analyze my dreams. The eyes
of people who hate me might be
spiders crawling on my hands,
or snails that leave their shells,
but I will not allow their acidic
tongues to touch me. I believe
in ghosts only now that her blue
eyes stick to me like humidity.

I will not outgrow my spite,
though I read books that instruct
me to. No, I'll always lie with my
sleep beside me like a knife.
I forgot my spite, once, only
to wish I had not: He lay me
upon the bed, crossed my arms
across my chest, then fell to me,
pressing a book between us.

I never lie in repose. I am not
a portrait. But I think so still
my joints ache. One day, he
shall not be the same (as I have

never been the same), and we
shall read upon his stone a verse
attributed to my name. This
is my foresight and my fright,
blooming red in his eye's white.

III

PLEASE

Repeating the word *Please, please, please*
don't call me. Voice stern, yet slightly frantic.
I imagine myself a heroine bound, her dress
torn at the neck (purity bitten at), whispering
to her lover through the door's crack, *Please*

go away—they'll kill you. The rewinding
tape on the answering machine: *Please, please,*
please don't call. When I think of appearing
at your door, a rival's face swells in its opening,
her hands real at my neck, my collar ripping, knees

scraping your stairs. *Don't ever show your face*
at this house again. I suck on each word like a stone.
I sift through foreign coins in a drawer.
They're made of a metal impossible to destroy—
dreadful currency. Is it us again, bound by a shared

peril? *She'll never find us out.* You considered
the secret sunk, a body defaced, wrapped in plastic,
weighted with stone and dumped into the sea between
us, a brick at its bottom. Let my voice raise the wreck
of that body. Let the people of your city crowd

around its sodden form, try to guess the name
of its face so bloated and torn. Let them know
we stood by the North Sea. Let a reporter establish
the exact location. And let your wife speak—
the arm she raises she raises in grief, the hand

she opens strikes your face. You, by the ocean,
saying *Please, please don't stop.* Well, I won't.

I'll announce what was fact, but is now suspicion.
I'm not the sunken ship, the unidentified body,
the kissed mouth, the product of your revision.

BOILING ROCKS

I.

The object is not to make a broth from rocks,
but to pure their bodies, scald off salt and dirt.
Sea-smoothed and silent, carried from coast
to stove, they weigh the pot, dark bodies now
as hot as the flames that leap from blue to orange.
They are honeymoon rocks, rocks that stop
my heart for envy of their salt knowledge.
Tears for them are nothing, they who lie
quiet in the pot, sleek and limpid as eyes.

II.

The object was to make a broth with rocks.
As the gas flowered blue beneath the pot,
I chopped onions at a table, stopping
just once to call his name. I began with limbs
and skin, melted them into the lathering pot.
The heart wasn't hard to unearth from his chest,
once my fingers grasped that slippery rock.
I saved the eyes for last, clinking them into
a bowl: blue jewels to roll upon the tongue.

III.

Poor rocks, outlasting the ocean's salty scratch,
ground in its mouth only to be spat back.
What seas' floors have you rolled along,
what tangles of inky weed have caught you
in their wrath, how was it to know the sea
would always take you back? Then feet landed

on you, eyes fell to you, and hands snatched
to drop you into a sack. You will never see
the sea again, never be moved as it moved you.

DISCIPLINE, ABANDON

I.

Everything here is made of wood, the floors
we move across amber with sun's sinking.
Our liquored evenings subtle then strong,
light drunk up till it's gone and our walking's

headlong. At night the walls bruise us. *Explain
these marks,* the morning asks. Though I blame
the house, I anticipate evening, the glass's cool
mouth against my mouth. The way the moon

stares back, confrontational. This house burned
down before we lived here. We still have ghosts
with us. Dead, the grandmother and infant.
They don't mind us in their house. Together:

I could be your mother, your sister, your friend,
but I'd rather be your lover, a song I dislike goes.

II.

What won't the house do in the meantime?
Compelled·by our drama, it sighs through
afternoons, anxious to open its cupboards
to evening. The house wants us moving inside

it, would have our every thought born in relation
to motion. My knuckle, your door. Your window,
my mouth. Disciplined at day, at night abandoned,
the ghosts offer their devotion. The house builds

itself around us. The house burns down for us.
When we walk the lawn late at night, arms looped,
circling its structure, we are faithful. Lights lure
us inside, floors beg to roll beneath us. Words

blurred, heady on rum, we lie all night like matches,
hazardous as kerosene in a barn, haywire with emotion.

OCEAN IS A WORD IN THIS POEM

One centimeter on the map represents one kilometer on the ground.
River I can cover with a finger, but it's not the water I resent.
   Ocean—
even the word thinks itself huge, and only because of what it
   meant.
I remember its lip on a road that ran along the coast of
   Portsmouth.

Waves tested a concrete brim where people stood to see how far
the water went. Sky was huge, but I didn't mind why. The sea
was too choppy and gray, a soup thick with salt and distance.
   Look,
sails are white as wedding dresses, but their cut is much cleaner.

No, I never planned to have a honeymoon by water, knew it'd
   tempt
me to leave your company, drop in. Ocean may allow boats to
   ride
its surface, but its word cannot anchor the white slip of this paper.
It cannot swallow the poem. Turbulence is on the wall. The
   map—

I would tear it, forget how I learned land's edge exists. I would
   sink
into the depth of past tense, more treacherous than the murk
   into
which our vessel went. Now when I pull down the map, eat its
   image
and paper, I'll swallow what wedding meant. Salt crusts my lips.

WORLD'S TALLEST DISASTER

These are the lines that will turn you inside out.
    A pocket pulled from your coat's side,
    exposing penny candies and the wad
    of bills you nicked from someone's locker.

These are the lines that will mark your brow.
    As your face contorts, eyes going wide.
    As you stutter, *I didn't know, I swear...*
    You smell of gasoline. Are those matches?

This stanza is the locked drawer in your desk.
    Has your wife managed to force it open?
    She holds the letter and reads aloud.
    Here follows a series of explosions.

And if this paper's a color, it's the pink welling
    from her hand's slap. Here's the pale
    hand you hold just over your mouth.
    Straighten up and stop your trembling.

Here's a picture of a building burning; worse
    than a slap, its skin's aflame. Look, orange
    windows! Can you see the arms waving?
    Why do your hands smell like gasoline?

And your skin, paler than any ghost, lets you get away
    with everything. The silver ring rests hot
    in your pocket, tarnishing into the same green
    as your iris. Your stare strokes a flame.

Here's the package I find when I get to the scene.
    Opening it, I see your lie, as big as a building.
    I light it with a match, study its burning.
    I watch its heat. Why does it feel like my body?

READING THE NEW SKY

In these intimate corridors: long, red rugs lie
like the tongues kept numb inside our mouths.
I do miss what's spoken, but forget why

in the midst of the sky's flashing outside. Late
day summer storm, how its x-ray terrifies.
Clouds so low they hug the road's long band

with shadow. Flash now, Light, press my eyes
with your gentle strangeness. I meant to take
the sky here and play it as lover, but what use

do I have for metaphor? It always placed a thing
between me and another. More familiar nights,
I thought myself and myself sleep's only equation.

Dreams did not rest me, grew from streets
that directed me, roads that drove themselves.
What I lay beside was never human: truth was,

I preferred to consider it monster. In these intimate
quarters, I need a drink—not this rain, not his kiss,
but the real thing: something strong enough to make

my sense thick. It's too real to find myself sober.
Before I'd have said: *the Moon slides back over*
a sky cloud-thick, my eye grows wide with it.

Why have I likened everything to element? Now
to be reconciled, to acknowledge a lie: it's not
the sky that has such terrible, beautiful weather.

THE LOCAL BLIND

1.

Avoiding the pair of blind men walking along the street,
edged up against the brick wall so their sticks miss me,
I notice the mailboxes, blue and American, standing like
sentries of my life, offering their wide lips to drop
word's parcel into.

2.

No one does not know me here. The frown on my pale
face has become a customary occurrence along this street.
Though the blind men cannot see it, they sense it, poke
their sticks in my direction.

3.

The blind men hear the siren but don't shrink as its blue
steadily caresses walls and streets, making black asphalt
blue-black. My love

4.

spoke of the town with admiration. Why can't I remember
just what he said, caressing its features with fond words?
Narrow, narrow, they must have been thinking

5.

when they built this town. Small minds liking small, small
definition of metropolis. My love's hands were useless,
he had no ambition. I'd spoon his eyes out, offer their
blueness to the blind men, who (taking one each) would
surely make better use of them.

6.

Maybe the blind men live in this town because it's easy
to get around. But if either had vision, I'd bet my savings
they'd take the next bus out. Money, money I saved so I
could see my love. When we agreed to meet in this town.

7.

The town knows I mourn him. The sky does too, with its
serious weather. Everything remembers how my hair hung
over his face and he breathed the smoke of its veil.

8.

I moved here so he could touch my features.

9.

And so I could search his features, the way I imagine
the blind men search their own in the final, private dark
of their rooms.

10.

My long looks tap down the street, poke crevices, search
dangerous curbs. At night I take out the letters he never
sent and read them with my fingertips.

THE NEGATIVE ELEMENT

It's time those houses were between us. Let us choose their
    residents.
You'll say, *Quiet ones,* but I want undesirable tenants.
All nine houses, a neighborhood. Let's make it a bad one.

Your house and mine at either end of it.

Couples who fight all night, scream at four in the morning at a
    dog
that won't stop barking—walls and halls smeared with
    fingerprints:
let their porches stay lit till dawn, trash cramming their doorways.

Though those houses were far from one another.

Though they rarely pay their rent, it's impossible to make them
    leave.
A loophole in the lease makes it their right. Was that sound
a laugh or a cry? Whatever the noise, it's close to pain.

Though we moved each year a great distance.

In each of the houses where you read those stories to me at night,
tales that sent me off to sleep with notions of wrong and right,
children discover what I once scrawled on dark closet walls.

Though those houses existed in a separate order.

Unkempt children spill out at night, armed with a menacing
    boredom.
Their varying ages wear my face in its various stages of
    development.
They make up for the fact you never took pictures.

Now that those houses stand together.

Your eyes wide all night. Will they discover the attraction
of your immaculate lawn? Is that your car's windshield they
    break?
Once they get in, they'll see it's neat as a pin. Nothing for them
    to take.

They'll find the rich are careful like that.

Let us latch the locks behind us. Now we sit in our separate
    houses,
behind our open papers, stirring cocktails as sirens astound us.
We'll share this discomfort as we could not share rooms.

All our nine houses like one fear between us.

BREAKFAST IN BED

It's not a sullen woman carrying.
It's not a tray being carried.
No bacon or eggs, no wreath of steam hanging
above a dark pool of coffee.

Whatever it is about morning
perhaps I like best knowing
where I am waking. I painted this room yellow
so I'd immediately recognize

my surroundings. But now I think I'm waking
inside a flower, fuzzed with pollen,
sneezing the phlegm of dream.
I must not love you if I don't dream

of loving you, I must not love anyone
if I dream of no one, but now that I have
your attention—for so long I've desired your attention—
let me tell you what it's like to kill

someone in a dream. Perhaps you know.
Well, then, let me tell you what
it's like for me. It is satisfying, terrifying,
terrifyingly satisfactory. And strange to find I know

the use of both knife and noose.
And you, who once lay like a little
bird in the crook of my arm (a man, a child, a lover!)—
to think I had your neck so close

and didn't take that moment.
I was so gone then, I mean in the mind,
that I couldn't look a disaster in the face
without saying I wanted a little kiss, just a little—

and then my hands would crawl
toward buttons—yes, yes, you know
what I'm speaking of, don't you?
In dreams, murder is art, sex is art, and art

is so extraordinary. Sometimes I'll speak a verse
more musical than music. Ecstasy.
But here we need something more concrete,
don't you think, love? The trembling

pulse, the bluest vein on your neck,
your sharp cry. A cry as if crushed,
wouldn't you say? It was yours, don't you have
something to say about it? What can

we say about coupling? By now
you'll find it boring, how you walked.
One foot, another foot: the entire city
could hear you moving down

my private street. When I lost
myself losing you—or perhaps I mean I lost you
when you lost me—I'd look for
you everywhere in dreams, trailing

my various paraphernalia: bottles
of almond-scented powder, a lady's
pearl-handled derringer, scarves
knotted together...now I wake to saffron

walls, pure air, light like streams
of cleanest water, a paradise of nonremberance,
clean hands and white sheets—but then
(something happened) my certain failure.

SPECTACULAR

And which way went the lovers, shocked
by sun palming their heads, hair electric
against the green drowse of lawn. Where

did the lovers head, a herd unto themselves,
roving toward stream bank, tumbling into
a cusp of green, sighing at a mountainside

view—always seeking another visage.
Hand in hand in hand she rubs, he thrums.
The story I would have: she throttles,

he withers. True story, she rubs, he grows.
Churn, churn, the engine of her fist, smooth
grease of her palm. Lovers, what you want

is what you want. You take no pleasure
at the other's face taking pleasure. And blue
the sky looks, like an egg you once spied

in a tiny nest—when you were a child
who liked to tear nature apart. Under blue light
you walk, eyes like diamonds, through

a yard struck with the bright of one peacock.
And when you go natural, run soft and flushed,
you tend to your imperfections—as hands polish

a knob, quick silver strokes, so mutual you
gleam. I glare like dislocated architecture.
The iris set in my head: black camera.

The skies are mad and storm to starry foam,
as I watch Spectacular you rolling on lawns,
asphyxiated by yourselves who are no ones.

CRY HEARD, FAR OFF

A prehistoric noise saws the air.
Will someone please help that creature?
The silver dome of the Elephants' House,
clouded in drizzle, is closer to this house
than other exhibits, but that ancient noise
cannot be theirs. Gray against gray,
the day will not unsettle.

City trees clump, stuporous in grinding
atmosphere. Will someone please help
that creature? It sounds up high, caught
in the traffic of trees. At its cry the dog's
ears prick. Now she moves her length
along the door anxiously. Struck it sounds,
stuck and unhelped.

It sounds up high, caught in the traffic
of air. It is time, I know, to discover
what creatures are housed there. But, Zoo:
I hesitate, I do not like to see a cage.
Though that screech: a noise bent like a saw
to split dull afternoon. I would have it high,
trafficked by trees.

I know it is time I discover the creature
large enough to raise that noise, feathered.
How does it preen, where does it sleep,
what sorts of things do they give it to eat?
Its noise says it is caught and uncaught.
Now the noise has stopped. Someone replaces
a cage to its creature.

CIGARILLO

The visit of a body. Ants gathered sugar
    along the kitchen counter. Their bounty was significant.
        But a moon ought to be red, too ripe for the sky.
            Instead, it lay a calm hand on the body.

By the door's unsealed edge, a chill found entrance.
    But a moon ought to be full. Instead, it was half.
        It hung like a low-watt bulb, gave just enough light to read
            lips by. Enough that it and the lit tip of the cigarillo

were all right to see the body by. In the half light,
    the belly was clean bone almost. The skin so young,
        I thought *soprano*. Rare to have a visitor call, strange
            to be overcome. But a moon ought to open for occasion.

Should I have called up the whole sky, interrogated
    constellations? No, it wasn't summer enough for flowers,
        even in the sky. But the moon was up so why
            wouldn't it attend to the evening? So my selfishness

would have stars fly like tears from a tossing head—
    but, no, the stomach was like pearl, the bed inhabited.
        The moon should have been as wide as the eyes were blue.
            Even if I couldn't see either through the smoke

from the cigarillo, which waved gray arms like ghosts
    in the room. I've had the sky in my grasp before, squinted
        hard to make a star shoot—but I was stunned before bareness,
            skin breathing its paleness. If the weather were in concert,

the perfection might have been bearable. The cigarillo's lit
    tip kissed darkness. It was a shrill moment, the touch
        of finger to tendon. In the yard, a leaf opened slowly.
            Sweet. The ants took to their path on the counter.

THE READERSHIP

I suppose must have been orbiting all the time
I've spent bent at this desk, unaware of its presence
as those victims of alien abductions, who claim
they were taken on board, experimented upon,

and gently replaced to their beds. Or the readership
may be hovering, held in a flight pattern, endlessly
repeating figure-eights, everyone on board desperate
for the captain's reassuring announcement

they'll make their connecting flights. Or perhaps
it's one of those massive sea vessels that looks
so grand from the shore, same as the ferry I saw
cutting its shape on the Mediterranean's edge,

when I was young and traveled with a notebook.
When to follow a map was to learn a finger's width
could mark the hours it'd take for us to get there.
Fellow passenger, companion, friend, perhaps when

you were sitting beside me your mind was really
on the readership. Maybe that could explain your
sudden disappearance: Mysterious as those lights
in late night skies no one can prove or identify.

Perhaps the readership prepares to land, and you
are among its passengers, presently ripping
at a bag of peanuts the flight attendants provide.
If this is so, I offer a goodly signal, words radiating

redness, radio towered. Much like a lighthouse
casts its warning to the morass of sea, I simply ask
that you heed me. Gentle barge, it does not matter
if you listen, it does not concern me. It's too late

for you to put the book down, cancel the flight,
concede you were always terrible at planning.
When you arrive, hold fast to your belongings.
The purse slashers in my poems have more

than your money on their unsubtle minds. I'll speak
for my life when I say I'm glad you have arrived.
I've waited like a starving country, arms heaped
with hand-worked goods I'll sell you at a native's price.

And if the readership does not exist? Perhaps
it's only intriguing as a conspiracy theory—
how I want to believe in it, as if it will provide
the answer for everything that's gone awry.

Sue Driskell

Cate Marvin was born in Washington, D.C. She received her B.A. from Marlboro College in Vermont, and holds two M.F.A.s: one from the University of Houston in poetry, the other from the Iowa Writers' Workshop in fiction. She has been awarded scholarships to attend both Bread Loaf and Sewanee Writers' Conferences. Her poems have appeared in such magazines as *New England Review, The Antioch Review, The Paris Review, The Georgia Review*, and *Ploughshares*, among others. She is currently a Ph.D. candidate in English at the University of Cincinnati.